W9-AAZ-069

VIDEO ECONOMICS

Every time you buy something you make an economic choice. **Economics** is the system of making and buying things that answer your needs and wants. Chester's friend Tamara has a **want**: a movie! Chester helps her make her choice by explaining why she is a "**consume**r" wrestling with "**supply and demand**."

WHO ARE THE ECONOMIC CONSUMERS?

CHESTER AND TAMARA ARE STARRING IN A STORY CALLED

ECONOMIC CHOICE

NOW PLAYING

WHAT DID YOU JUST CALL ME?!!

THE **CONSUMER**! YOU USE GOODS AND SERVICES. YOU WANT THINGS, SO YOU **BUY** THEM FROM BUSINESSES.

CAN I HAVE A COOL WEB TO GRAB THINGS? HOW ABOUT A GIANT CLAW!

NONONO! **THESE** ARE THE DEVICES YOU WILL USE TO GET WHAT YOU WANT AND NEED...

BOYD '02

BARTER

IN BARTER, YOU TRADE GOODS AND SERVICES WITHOUT USING MONEY. THIS IS THE WAY EARLY SOCIETES IN THE WORLD WORKED.

MONEY

WHAT IF SOMEONE DOESN'T WANT YOUR AX OR YOUR COW'S MILK? YOU NEED SOMETHING THAT CAN BE TRADED ANY TIME: MONEY. MONEY IS A CURRENCY THAT HAS A CERTAIN TRADING VALUE.

DEBT

PEOPLE WITHOUT COWS OR MONEY CAN STILL GET THINGS BY PROMISING TO PAY FOR THEM LATER AND ASKING PRETTY, PRETTY, PRETTY PLEASE.

I.O.U.

CREDIT

CREDIT CARDS ARE A WAY TO USE DEBT. A PERSON WHO CHARGES AN ITEM ON THEIR CARD PROMISES TO PAY FOR IT LATER, IN MONTHLY PAYMENTS.

MONTHLY BILL

I HAVE SOME CASH MONEY I GOT FOR MY BIRTHDAY. I CAN USE THAT TO BUY THE MOVIE I WANT!

THE NEXT QUESTION: WHERE CAN YOU FIND THE RIGHT MOVIE AT THE BEST PRICE? WHO WILL SELL IT TO YOU?

VIDEO ROW! LET'S GO THERE NEXT!

WHAT IS YOUR OPPORTUNITY COST?

WELL, TAMARA, WHAT WILL YOUR ECONOMIC CHOICE BE? YOU CAN'T BUY ALL THE STUFF IN ALL THREE STORES. THEIR GOODS AND SERVICES ARE LIMITED — AND SO IS YOUR MONEY.

I HAVE $15 WITH ME FROM MY BIRTHDAY. ON SATURDAY I WILL GET $5 FOR MY WEEKLY ALLOWANCE. SHOULD I BUY SOMETHING TODAY OR WAIT?

choice #1

BUY NOTHING TODAY. WAIT A WEEK UNTIL YOU HAVE ENOUGH MONEY TO BUY THE MOVIE YOU WANT.

choice #2

BUY TODAY. THIS MOVIE IS NOT YOUR FIRST CHOICE, AND IT IS ON A TAPE, WHICH WILL NOT LAST AS LONG AS A DVD.

choice #3

BUY ONE, TWO, OR THREE PRE-VIEWED TAPES TODAY. THESE ARE NOT YOUR FIRST CHOICE EITHER, AND THE TAPE QUALITY MAY BE BAD.

THIS IS **opportunity cost**. THE PRICE OF A MOVIE IS NOT JUST THE PRICE IN DOLLARS. IT IS ALSO WHAT YOU MUST DO TO GET THE DOLLARS AND WHAT YOU DON'T BUY WHEN YOU MAKE YOUR CHOICE.

I'LL BUY A USED VIDEOTAPE OF SPONGEROB TV EPISODES. THAT'S ONLY $5.

WHAT IS YOUR OPPORTUNITY COST?

I DON'T GET TO BUY "MONSTERS, CO." TODAY, AND I HAVE TO WAIT TWO MORE WEEKS TO GET ENOUGH ALLOWANCE TO BUY "ICED AGE."

YOU COULD JUST **SAVE** YOUR MONEY. WAITING ONE MORE WEEK WOULD GET YOU ENOUGH FOR THE DVD!

YOU SOUND LIKE MY MOM AND DAD.

HOW ABOUT WASHING SOME CARS? RAKING LEAVES? I KNOW SOMEONE WHO PAYS $10 FOR POWERWASHING THEIR SIDEWALKS! END

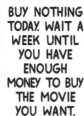

MONEY AROUND THE MALL

Chester follows some **money** around a mall as it changes from **cash** to a **check** to a **bank account** to a **credit card**. It is all money, but each form of money has its own uses and advantages. See if you can spot all the magic changes in this economic treasure hunt!

HOW DO YOU TURN CHICKS INTO CHECKS?

SO, LISA, WHAT IS THE FIRST THING YOU'LL BUY WITH YOUR NEW **COINS AND CURRENCY**?

FOOD!

Chicken Nuggets on a Stick

HEY GUYS!

HI, JOSH. CAN I HAVE ONE STICK?

SURE. THAT'S $2.15.

THANKS! I'M GOING OVER TO J-BEE TOYS NOW. SEE YA, CHESTER!

AND THAT'S ALL FOR **ME**, FOLKS! TIME TO TURN IN THE **CASH** FROM THE REGISTER.

IT ALL ADDS UP, JOSH. GOOD JOB — HERE IS YOUR **PAYCHECK**.

WHOO HOO!

PRESTO! NOTICE HOW LISA'S CASH TURNED INTO A DIFFERENT PIECE OF PAPER?

Brownes and no/100 ——— Dec. 21 19 99 2790

50.00 ——→ DOLLARS

A **CHECK** IS A PAPER TELLING A **BANK** TO PAY SOMEONE ELSE THE AMOUNT YOU WRITE.

BOYD '99

PEOPLE USE CHECKS TO PAY FOR EXPENSIVE THINGS. CARRYING A CHECK IS SAFER THAN CASH BECAUSE IT IS WORTHLESS UNTIL YOU WRITE AN AMOUNT AND YOUR SIGNATURE ON IT!

THIS PIECE OF PAPER IS WORTH $50 TO ME!

BUT ONLY IF YOU TAKE IT TO ...

THE BANK!

Whew! I WISH THIS PLACE HAD A MOVING CRABWALK!

NEXT: YOU CAN BANK ON IT

CHESTER THE CRAB
WHY IS A BANK BETTER THAN A JAR?

Panel 1: SO, JOSH, WHAT KINDS OF GOODIES AND SERVICES ARE YOU GETTING WITH YOUR PAYCHECK?

BANK

NOTHING — YET!

Panel 2: I'M PUTTING MY CHECK INTO MY **SAVINGS** ACCOUNT AT THE BANK. I'M WAITING UNTIL I HAVE ENOUGH MONEY TO PAY THE **PRICE** OF A MOUNTAIN BIKE!

OOH, THAT'S A **GOODY!**

PLEASE SIGN YOUR DEPOSIT SLIP, MR. PECK.

Panel 3: HOW LONG HAVE YOU BEEN SAVING?

A FEW MONTHS. WHAT'S COOL IS THE BANK PAYS **ME** 4% INTEREST. WHEN I TAKE OUT MY MONEY IN A FEW WEEKS, I'LL HAVE MY $300 PLUS $20 EXTRA FROM THE INTEREST. I **LOVE** WHEN PEOPLE GIVE ME MONEY!

SAVINGS RECORD

BOYD '99

Panel 4: DO YOU KNOW **WHY** THE BANK GIVES YOU THE EXTRA 4%?

WHO CARES?! IT WORKS FOR ME! LATER, BUD.

STAR

Panel 5: THE BANK GIVES JOSH INTEREST AS A REWARD FOR KEEPING HIS MONEY THERE INSTEAD OF IN A JAR UNDER HIS BED. THE BANK GETS TO USE HIS MONEY WHILE HE ISN'T. IT'S LIKE THE BANK IS RENTING JOSH'S MONEY.

Panel 6: IN A JAR, JOSH'S MONEY DOES NOT HELP ANYONE ELSE. BUT THE BANK CAN LOAN IT TO OTHER PEOPLE FOR AWHILE. ...LIKE SHAWNA.

CHANGE-O!

I'M GETTING MY OWN CREDIT CARD!

HOW DO YOU BUY NOW, PAY LATER?

CONGRATULATIONS, MISS BAKER. YOU'VE BEEN APPROVED FOR A **CREDIT CARD** FROM 1ST BANK.

WHERE DO I SIGN?

BASICALLY, WE'RE **LOANING** YOU MONEY WHENEVER YOU USE THE CARD. (WE GIVE YOU MONEY OTHERS GAVE TO US.)

WHERE DO I SIGN?

WE ASK THAT AT THE END OF EACH MONTH YOU PAY FOR THE GOODS AND SERVICES YOU CHARGED ON THE CARD. IF YOU DON'T, YOU PAY US 18% INTEREST ON THE UNPAID AMO.

WHERE DO I SIGN?!

HERE.

YEAH, BABY!

AND SIGN THE BACK OF THE CARD, PLEASE.

Alphonso McFunstere

HAVE YOU NOTICED THAT SPENDING CASH DOES NOT NEED A SIGNATURE OF YOUR NAME — BUT SPENDING OTHER KINDS OF MONEY **DOES**? CHECKS AND CREDIT CARDS DEPEND ON **TRUST**. PEOPLE NEED TO KNOW YOUR MONEY CAN BE TURNED BACK INTO **CASH**. YOUR SIGNATURE IS YOUR PROMISE THAT IT CAN.

BLOYD '99

THIS GREAT, MOM! NOW I CAN GET THIS DRESS FOR THE KWANZAA PARTY!

GAB

SHAWNA, WHY ARE YOU USING CREDIT INSTEAD OF CASH?

IF I WAIT TO BUY THIS WITH MY GRANDMA'S KWANZAA GIFT (**CASH**!), THE PARTY WILL BE OVER. THE CREDIT CARD LETS ME GET A DRESS **NOW** AND PAY FOR IT **AFTER** I GET GRANDMA'S GIFT AT THE PARTY!

ALL *THAT*!

SHAWNA, YOU GOT THE CREDIT YOU DESERVE!

NEXT: CA$HING IN

CAREER RESOURCES

What would you like to be when you grow up? Chester helps his friend Darryl think about that by looking at some jobs from 100 years ago. He also show how the jobs we do use **human resources**, **natural resources**, and **capital resources**.

CHESTER THE CRAB
WHAT ARE ECONOMIC RESOURCES?

HI, DARYLLE! CAN I SWING AFTER YOU?

NOPE. I AM DOING MY HOMEWORK.

OH, YEAH? WHAT FOR, SOME SCIENCE EXPERIMENT? SOMETHING ON FORCE OR MOMENTUM?

I AM FINDING A HUMAN RECESS!

UMM, I THINK YOUR TEACHER MIGHT MEAN "RESOURCE."

WHAT IS A "RESOURCE?"

THEY COME IN THREE TYPES:

NATURAL RESOURCES
THINGS FOUND IN NATURE: WATER, WOOD, AIR, SUN, VERY SMALL ROCKS.

HUMAN RESOURCES
PEOPLE WORKING TO PRODUCE GOODS AND SERVICES: FARMERS, BUILDERS, PAINTERS.

CAPITAL RESOURCES
THINGS MADE BY PEOPLE AND USED TO PRODUCE OTHER GOODS AND SERVICES: HAMMERS, COMPUTERS, TRUCKS.

OH. WELL, CAN YOU HELP ME FIND SOME EXAMPLES? I NEED THEM BY NEXT MONDAY.

NEXT: DOCTOR! DOCTOR!

BOYD '01

14

WHAT DID DOCTORS USE IN 1901?

THIS IS A TIME OF CHANGE FOR DOCTORS. OLD-FASHIONED HERB MEDICINES AND HOME REMEDIES ARE SLOWLY GIVING WAY TO MODERN MEDICINES.

DARYLLE, LET'S SEE IF WE CAN FIND SOME RESOURCES FOR YOUR HOMEWORK.

SHOULD I PRESCRIBE THIS?!?!

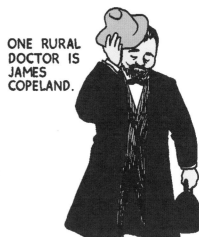

ONE RURAL DOCTOR IS JAMES COPELAND.

IS HE GOING TO WORK?

THIS IS HIS OFFICE! HE MAKES HOUSE CALLS. DR. COPELAND CARRIES MEDICINES IN THAT SADDLE BAG.

RELAX, JIM. A PLASTER WILL REDUCE YOUR NAUSEA.

THIS OLD-STYLE CURE WILL CAUSE A NASTY BLISTER TOO!

OK, DARYLLE, CAN YOU PICK OUT EXAMPLES OF THREE RESOURCES?

WELL, DR. COPELAND HIMSELF IS THE **HUMAN RESOURCE**. A DOCTOR PRODUCES A SERVICE: TAKING CARE OF SICK PEOPLE.

HIS **NATURAL RESOURCE** IS THAT PLASTER STUFF HE PUTS ON A PATIENT.

HE HAS A LOT OF **CAPITAL RESOURCES**. HIS TOOLS INCLUDE HIS SADDLEBAG FOR CARRYING MEDICINE AND HIS STETHOSCOPE.

OWIE! THAT STINGS!

P.U.!

NEXT: BEACH

HOW DID PEOPLE VACATION IN 1901?

CHESTER AND FIRST-GRADER DARYL'LE ARE LOOKING FOR RESOURCES.

LET'S HIT A RESORT!

BOYD '01

GEORGE CHRISTIAN GUVERNATOR IS PROMOTING HIS NEW "BEACH PARK."

COME IN, BOYS! SIT DOWN FOR MY BIG "SHORE DINNER" OF SEA-FOOD, 50 CENTS!

RIDE MY MERRY-GO-ROUND!

AAAAAHH

HEY, SON, NICE DANCING! GO TO MY DANCE ROOM TO HEAR MY BAND!

DARYLLE, CAN YOU SEE STRAIGHT TO PICK OUT SOME RESOURCES??

Ahh...ulp! I.. woah!

I GUESS GUVERNATOR IS TAKING ADVANTAGE OF **NATURAL RESOURCES.** HIS RESORT LETS PEOPLE ENJOY THESE RIVERS.

HIS RESORT USES MANY MAN-MADE TOOLS (**CAPITAL RESOURCES**): TRAINS, MERRY-GO-ROUNDS, AND INSTRUMENTS.

AND GUVERNATOR HIMSELF IS ABOUT THE WILDEST **HUMAN RESOURCE** I HAVE EVER SEEN!

VISIT MY SHOOTING GALLERY! SODA FOUNTAIN! PHOTO STUDIO! PLAY GAMES! WIN PRIZES! COME ONE COME ALL!!

NEXT: LAWMEN

WHAT WERE TEACHER RESOURCES IN 1901?

CHESTER AND FIRST-GRADER DARYLLE ARE LOOKING FOR RESOURCES IN 1901...

THIS HAS BEEN FUN COLLECTING EXAMPLES. I AM READY TO GO BACK TO SCHOOL.

OK!

OOP!?!

ANOTHER STUDENT! GOOD. I TRUST YOU HAVE FINISHED HARVESTING ON YOUR FAMILY'S FARM?

THIS IS A RURAL SCHOOL.

I AM THE TEACHER, GENEVIEVE COCKRILLE. WE ARE DOING A SPELLING LESSON. SPELL "FRIEND."

:GULP: IS THIS FOR REAL?

RURAL TEACHERS IN 1901 FOCUS ON READING, SPELLING, AND A LITTLE MATH.

YOU NEED AN "E." REMEMBER: A FRIEND IS A FRIEND UNTIL THE "END." I WILL SWITCH YOU SO YOU REMEMBER.

YOW!

CAN I GO BACK TO STUDYING RESOURCES!?

FRIND

BBOYD '01

SURE! ECONOMICS IS IMPORTANT. IT HELPS YOU DECIDE WHAT JOB YOU WANT TO DO SOMEDAY.

WELL, BEING A TEACHER WOULD MAKE ME A **HUMAN RESOURCE.**

CAPITAL RESOURCES ARE SCHOOL BUILDINGS AND DESKS AND BOOKS FOR THE STUDENTS.

AND THE **NATURAL RESOURCE** HERE IS HER CHALK — AND THAT BIG STICK SHE'S GOT!!

I AM DONE WITH THIS HOMEWORK! BYE! END

CHAPTER 4

THE TAX HUNTER

Taxes are a part of your **citizenship** in your **country, state,** or **local government**. We pay different kinds of **taxes** so that our government can do different kinds of things for us. Adults pay most of the taxes, but even kids can pay a sales tax on things they buy at a store. Chester hunts down some strange animals that remind him of the different kinds of taxes in America.

WHO IS The Tax Hunter?

YOU HAD BETTER STILL BE HUNTING CROCODILES, MISTER!

NAAH! CROCS ARE OCKERS NOW!

TODAY I AM HUNTING FOR SOMETHING FAR MORE ELUSIVE AND HARD TO UNDERSTAND...

TAXES!

TAXES?! YOU MEAN, LIKE, **MONEY**??

THAT'S RIGHT, MATE! SOME GOVERNMENT AGENTS HAVE HIRED ME TO BRING IN THE QUID!

TAXES ARE MONEY THAT PEOPLE ARE SUPPOSED TO PAY THEIR GOVERNMENT TO PROVIDE SERVICES SUCH AS FIRE DEPARTMENTS, LIBRARIES...

YAH, ONLY SOME SHONKY PEOPLE DON'T DO THEIR CIVIC DUTY AND PAY ON TIME. SO IT'S UP TO ME TO...

HEY!! THERE'S A TAX NOW!!

NEXT: PROPERTY PYTHONS

CHESTER THE CRAB
WHAT KIND of PROPERTY IS TAXED?

CHESTER IS TRACKING THROUGH THE BRUSH WITH

The Tax Hunter.

SO YOU'RE OUT HERE LOOKING FOR MONEY THAT GOES TO THE **GOVERNMENT.**

RIGHT! THERE ARE LOTS OF DIFFERENT KINDS OF TAXES. TAKE A SQUIZZ AT THIS ONE!

PROPERTY TAX

THERE ARE TWO KINDS:

REAL PROPERTY TAXES ARE BASED ON THE LAND OR BUILDINGS THAT A PERSON OR BUSINESS OWNS.

PERSONAL PROPERTY TAXES ARE TAKEN FROM THE VALUE OF SOMEONE'S MACHINERY, CARS, OR THINGS THAT ARE TEMPORARY OR MOVABLE.

IF YOU OWN A HOME OR CAR, THIS TAX CAN COST YOU BIG BIKKIES!

THESE GUYS ARE WORTH A FEW ZACKS!! WE'LL DELIVER THEM TO **LOCAL GOVERNMENT.**

THANKS, TAX HUNTER! WE'LL USE THESE TO PAY FOR OUR CITY'S SCHOOLS, LIBRARIES, STREETS, AND POLICE AND FIRE DEPARTMENTS.

NEXT: *Come Sale Away*

CHESTER THE CRAB
WHEN IS A SALES TAX COLLECTED?

NEXT: *income over*